Plan
Like You Mean It !

Karen L Tarango

<u>DEDICATION</u>

I dedicate this book to my sister
Sharon Tovar-Davis.
Planning with meaning
allowed us to create
new memories
when we needed it most.

1

ACKNOWLEDGEMENTS

I want to give thanks to the
The Fresno Planner Girls group
for their inspiration and
friendship.
I never knew there were others
like me! It is wonderful to have
like minded friends sharing the
same passion.
I also want to thank
Haley Kyriss
for taking the time to read my
manuscript during editing and to
give her insightful thoughts.

I give all the glory to God
who gave me the idea to write
this book in the first place.
The Master planner who has good
plans for me.

"For I know the plans I have for
you," declares the Lord,
"plans to prosper you and not to
harm you, plans to give you a
hope and a   future."

Jeremiah 29:11

CONTENTS

Introduction

My planning journey began about thirty years ago. While in college I had the standard student calendar to schedule my classes and exam dates. It was a few years later that I laid my eyes on a Franklin Covey planner. They were expensive but the leather covers were more than I could resist. I soon realized it wasn't just a nice cover but a whole system created by Franklin Covey himself. However, I was too busy to really get into the Covey way of planning.

Gradually I began trying out other planners drawn in by their cute layouts and pretty colors. Yet never understanding that there was more to it than just writing in your day's plans.

I have always enjoyed organizing and planning. So when my sister told me about a local group of ladies who met every other month to work on their planners, I was ecstatic! I didn't know there were other people like me who loved to plan. It was during one of those meet-ups where I was introduced to the Erin Condren planner. I loved the idea that you could personalize it in a variety of ways!

I quickly ordered one and all the extras. Then two years later I discovered the tiny Hobonichi Weeks planner! So small and perfect purse size. This is what I currently use.

I can truly appreciate all the different planners and their uniqueness. The creative ways of dressing up the pages with stickers and planner accessories are endless. But the truth is to be really satisfied with your planner to reach that "planner peace", you need to go deeper into your system. Which is what I hope to bring you in this book. So get out your highlighters and page markers and let's get reading!

Common Questions

When the planner bug hits you it can be so exciting! You rush to the store and touch all the pretty papers and try out the colorful pens. You look though countless, shiny, new planners until it is all overwhelming. Then end up leaving the store empty handed. We have all been there my friend. So let me begin by first answering a few common questions that most beginners have. It will help you to make those buying decisions easier.

What do I plan?

You may be thinking you don't have much going on in your life to warrant having a calendar or any type of fancy planner. Nothing could be father from the truth. We all have things we need to get done in our day. To make it simple, just schedule in the top three things that must get done that day. Write them down and check them off. For example, you could calendar your work schedule and days off. Another item could be doctor or dentists appointments. If your a student there is a lot you can plan.

From homework assignments to test dates. You can also write in when bills are due and your paydays. Again just pick three things to get started. You don't want to get overwhelmed with a packed planner.

There are so many planners to pick from, how do I choose?

Start out with a simple calendar. If your a woman you may want something you can toss in your purse or bag for on the go planning. Some people prefer to schedule right in their phone calendars and that's fine too.

Give it a few months before you jump into the more expensive planners and all the cute stickers out there. This way you can just focus on your system instead of all the decorations. Your system or method is the important part. Get that down before going further or purchasing a lot of things you may not need.

There is this mindset I believe people have, that if you have the cutest decorations or most expensive planner that you will be an organizing pro. Not true. The material things that we buy are just the icing on the cake. It's the system or method you use which is the key to a productive plan.

When do you plan?

Everyone will be different in the answer to this question. Some will plan on a Sunday evening before the week starts. Others in the middle of the week. Then there are those who plan as needed, when appointments are made or simply on the go.

More than likely there will be a mixture of all of the above. I plan once a week, on Monday's while I'm filming for my youtube channel. Then during the week there are things that come up to pop into my schedule. Its a dynamic process never static.

With that said, I do enjoy sipping coffee and going through my planner. Either to review what is coming up or to update and check off things that have passed. It relaxes me and I love looking at all the pretty decorations in my pages, not to mention photos.

What system do I use?

Everyone will be different. What works beautifully for one may not work for another. My system that I use is simple. I use a monthly, weekly, and daily layouts in a cohesive way. The things I have scheduled in my month I will transfer over into the week they occur.

I tend to work off my weekly pages. If I have a particularly busy day I will use my daily page. This is to keep me focused on all I have going on that day.

My system includes a lot of tracking. I track my daily workouts, the weather, what I eat and my writing plan for the day. This is the system that I came up with for me. When or if I want to move into another planner, my system would stay the same. Only the planner would change. Your system is the bones of your planning journey. It holds everything together. It may take a while to figure out what works best for you.

There will be tweaking and adjustments. Some ideas you will keep and others you will throw out until finally you have your own personal system that is tailored for your needs.

"Always plan ahead,
it wasn't raining
when Noah built the ark"
Richard Cushing

<u>Deep Planning</u>

What does it mean to plan deeply? Planning deeply is getting pass all the fluff and going deeper to spend your time on things and people that mean the most to you. By this I mean planning with purpose and meaning. Purpose is scheduling with the idea of an outcome. Where an action will be required. Where as planning with meaning is doing something that touches your soul. Such as, spending time with your grandchildren; it is meaningful to you. With that in mind, the goal is to schedule both types into your week.

Many years ago I found myself very stressed. I would look at my planner and would be over whelmed by how much I needed to get done. Yet I was the one making the schedule! After much prayer and thinking, I decided to put away my beautiful red, leather, planner for a season. Instead I printed out a single monthly sheet I got off the internet for free, it was plain and boring.

I only scheduled in book writing and ministry work. That's it, and it was so liberating! All my stress melted away. I didn't know it at the time but I was planning with purpose.

It was then that I realized what I had previously done that stressed me out. I would schedule in every little thing in my planner until I ran out of room. Not "everything" needed to be written down. Only important things that had meaning and purpose.

Finally I was done with this willy nilly way of planning. Now I had a new way and it was liberating! Planning with meaning and purpose will inherently bring focus into your life. You will become more productive and better able to accomplish your goals. You will also have more time with people you love.

Deep planning will give you a new perspective on what's truly important to you. You will also see your priorities fall into their proper place.

In the following pages I will take you step by step into deep planning. The first five steps will be about planning with purpose. What that means and how you can do that now. Then there will be five other steps on how to plan with meaning. You can incorporate this into your calendar immediately.

So lets get started!

Five Steps to Planning with Purpose

#1 Goals

Someone once said,

> *"A goal without a plan is just a wish"*

So the first step in planning with purpose is goals. They are the driving force in planning. Let me give you a practical example. Let's say this week I want to get five loads of laundry washed, dried, and put away. But I don't want to spend a day doing a mound of laundry.

Therefore, I turn this into a goal by breaking down the laundry into small manageable loads. Schedule in your week planner to do a single load of laundry every day. Don't forget to dry and put away the clothes as well. Then check it off your list. The next day do the same thing and continue through out the week. By the end of the week all five loads are done! With goals you can accomplish a lot. They truly are the driving force in planning with purpose.

The dictionary defines a goal as an aim of a desired result. You use it as a tool to get the results you want.

One item I scheduled in todays plan was to find out how many sugar grams I consumed today. So my goal for today is to count and add up all the sugar grams of sugar in my meals. Then at the end of the day I total it all up and have my answer.

You can also create a weekly or monthly goal. Maybe consider a one year or five year goal! In the same way these larger goals can be broken down into smaller ones. Just remember to think of them as a tool to get you the results you want. And this tool is a valuable asset to your planning process and success.

#2 Routine

The second step of planning with purpose is to write down your morning routine. Then keep that in your planner on your current day.

Why a morning routine?

Many reasons, such as getting those necessary things out of the way before you get started with your day. This also prevents distractions and procrastination.

Here is an example of a morning routine

1. Make coffee

2. Read Bible or devotional

3. Shower and get dressed

4. Feed the animals

5. Get the kids off to school

6. Tidy up kitchen

7. Start your day

Consistency is the key. The more you are consistent in your routine, the less likely you'll be distracted with the things on your list. A morning routine will teach you to stick faithfully to a plan. Which in the long run will cause you to be more successful with your goals! Then you will be free to move forward in your day because you've accomplished your routine.

A big hindrance which holds people back from a productive day is procrastination. But when you consistently go though your morning routine you break that procrastination cycle and are free to move forward.

You don't want to be a person who says, what if...What if I did follow my dreams? What if I did ask for that raise? What if I did go back to school? You see how procrastination can rob you of so much in life. It's more serious than we realize.

A written down morning routine is a powerful tool for you to implement in your planning. So if you don't already have one, create yours and insert it into your weekly layout so you can see it everyday. It won't be perfect so don't fuss over it too much. You can   adjust it a few times until you are happy with the list. It sets you up mentally for the day and we can all benefit from that!

Allen Lakein said *"Failing to plan is planning to fail."*

#3 Monthly layout

The third step of planning with purpose is utilizing your monthly layout. Use it to record time and day specific events or appointments. An example of a day specific event is a birthday. It lands on the same day every year. A time specific event would be a Dentist appointment at 3 pm. Here is a list below of what you could schedule in your monthly calendar.

* Monthly meetings

* Bank service fees

* Automatic withdrawals

* Out of town trips

* Classes / workshops

* Birthdays / anniversaries

* Weddings / funerals

* Parties

* Paydays

* Vacations

* Pet vaccination reminders
28

Once these are in place, it provides a big picture of your month at a glance. Therefore, you can better prepare for those events and nothing catches you by surprise. You can see what is coming up in the near future. I suggest setting up not only your current month but also the following month as well. Many times we need to schedule things a month or two ahead. This way you will be ready to do just that. Once you have all your monthly items written down, be sure to transfer them over to the exact day they will take place. Either in your weekly pages or daily pages. It is so nice to refer to the month page and see all that will be happening at a glance.

#4 Staying ahead

Step four is staying ahead of it all. Staying ahead of it all means scheduling in your appointments but also getting prepared for those appointments. Because there is more to planning than writing in your planner. It will allow you to better handle big events when you have the foresight to break them down into doable action steps. Fine tune your skills to think in a forward direction and the smaller steps to get there. With that said, not all the things you plan will warrant this foreword thinking.

For example; A wedding is a big event, and to simply write in "Wedding Day" on the date in your planner isn't enough to get the job done. If you are the one getting married you will have many steps to take to make that wedding day a reality. For instance, one step to schedule would be shopping for your wedding dress. Another would be a dress fitting appointment, and so on. Only preparation planning will make that wedding day a reality. Breaking it down into smaller steps and multiple appointments will keep you ahead of it all.

#5 Plan

This last step is make an appointment to plan. Every week, sit down with your planner, favorite pens, and something to drink. Review the coming week and schedule in any last minute appointments. Be sure to schedule this time with yourself weekly. And if you have a significant other it would be a good idea to coordinate your calendars. My husband and I do that once a month.

Often times I hear people say, "I forgot to write it in my calendar." Or "I didn't have time to write that down."

To avoid missing appointments or events, plan to plan. Do this when there is minimal distractions so you can think. Get comfortable and enjoy the process. Planning is suppose to be fun! Add some color to your pages and decorate with stickers. Include a favorite quote or bible verse. I find that when my planner pages are pretty I enjoy using them more.

Planning to plan will save you missed appointments or bill paying dates. If you stay on top of things it may even save you money! Whatever your situation is be sure to make time to plan. It will be one of the most important appointments in your week!

My Little Planner Poem
by Karen L.Tarango

Little planner, little planner,
full of paper and what nots
my favorite pens and sticky dots
Oh the stories you could tell
Highlighted plans
Here and now
But looking closer
Past the stickers and tape
Turn the pages of calendar dates
What would they see of you and
me?

Their eyes would gaze upon
My hopes and dreams
Magnificent goals unseen
Fresh starts and new beginnings
An open book to my heart
All my dreams from the start
All in my little planner,
little planner
Full of paper and what nots.

Five Steps to
Planning with Meaning

Now we move into five steps to planning with meaning. These are things that touch your soul. They have special significance and put a smile on your face. In short, they add depth and value to your planner because of what they mean to you.

"An hour of planning can save you 10 hours of doing."
Dale Carnegie

1. Quotes

Step one is to write through out your planner quotes or bible verses that inspire you. Personally I love a good quote. They can really motivate me and I enjoy putting them in my planner right where I can see them everyday. They range from funny quotes, to beautiful bible verses.

The idea is to have these positive sayings which you can read through out your week. We have enough troubles and negativity in the world, but it doesn't have to be that way in our planners.

Another idea you can use is to write down a compliment that someone gave you. How wonderful it would be to read that compliment every day! Especially if you are having a challenging week that kind word can do wonders for your soul.

There are many online shops that sell pages of quote stickers. They are easy to stick right in your planner. Of course you can write them in directly as well. The important thing is to incorporate them in your layouts.

"Plans are nothing:
Planning is everything"
Dwight D. Eisenhower

2. Vision Boards / Pages

The second step in planning with meaning is a vision board. Except you would create it on a page in your planner or add a page or two if you don't have the extra space. The idea is to write down your goals in a visually appealing way. First think of some goals you want to accomplish.

The fun part is finding photos or magazine images that represent your goals. Tape those down on your page. Next to those photos you would write down your goals and include all the details of what you want. There is no wrong way to create a vision board! If you want to know more, I recommend reading "Dream it. Pin it. Live it. Make Vision Boards Work For You." By Terri Savelle Foy. A wonderful book that will help you immensely! When you look at your vision page of goals, visualize yourself accomplishing them. Live it out in your mind, and don't give up!

3. Photos

The third step in planning with meaning is to add photos! Like that old adage, "A picture is worth a thousand words." When you add a photo to your layout it brings with it memories. A new sense of meaning and worth is embedded into your planner. Which once was a book of paper and ink, now bubbles over in memories and stories ready to be told once again.

If you have a tiny planner like me, don't be dismayed you can still fit in photos.

I have a mini printer from Canon called Ivy. Just download the app on your cell phone. From there it will sync to the mini printer ready to print mini photos for your layouts. You can make them as small as you want!

Personally I love adding a "photo of the week" to my weekly schedule. Then when looking back I have fun memories I won't soon forget. As an alternative you can add mementos to your page as well. Maybe movie ticket stubs, or some other paper mementos to remind you of an event. Get creative!

4. Personalize

The fourth step in planning with meaning is to personalize your planner. Go beyond decorations and color coding. Consider what you really need and make your planner work for you. If you need more pouches, get those in there. If you need more pockets, get those in there. Write a list of your top three needs then fill those needs. You will happier with your planner and more productive.

For me, I reserve a place in my weekly layout for a prayer list.

It keeps me focused on who I am praying for that week. I also needed room for multiple pens. A big pouch was the answer for me.

Think of your planner as working for you. What do you need out of it and how can you make that happen. It's a tool to help you be the most productive you can be in your day, week, and month. Sure it's nice to have a pretty planner but it is better to have a pretty planner that works for you. It may take some time to figure out what you need but it will be worth it as you schedule your life.

*"It takes as much energy to wish
as it does to plan."*
Eleanor Roosevelt

5. Word of the year

The fifth step in planning with meaning is to choose a word of the year. The idea is to pick a word that would be your theme or focus for the year. Here is an example; If you believe it is time for you to grow in all aspects of your life then your word may be, *grow or step up or stretch.*

As a reminder to yourself, write your word at the top of your monthly and weekly layout pages. To incorporate it more in your life you can journal about your word of the year and what it means to you. My word currently is *plan*. I truly need to plan out a lot this year and this keeps me focused on that reality.

"Unless commitment is made, there are only promises and hopes but no plans"
Peter F. Druker

Conclusion

There is more to planning than jotting down a schedule or making a list of to do's. There is a better way to get things done and free up your precious time. This discipline takes time to become a habit. So relax and enjoy the process, and don't forget to add some cute stickers along the way.

Planning with purpose and meaning can help make sense of all the "stuff" in your life. Separating the practical from the things that touch your soul. We need to give our schedules some balance then you will be on your way to a productive planned life.

Enjoy my friend.

A Note From The Author

Just a word about planners in general. Many people stress and worry about which planner to purchase. Is it the best one for me? Is it cute? Expensive? Can I personalize it? Is it portable? So many decisions!

What I suggest you focus on is your *system* or *method* of planning. Once you have that down you can easily move from planner to planner with out any problem. Because its not the planner that matters, its what you do with it that counts.

Happy planning!

-Karen